Economics and the
Christian Worldview

Economics and the Christian Worldview

Dave Arnott

Dave Arnott, Publisher
2019

First Printing: 2019

ISBN: 978-0-578-56724-2

Dave Arnott, Publisher
davea@dbu.edu | dvarnott@gmail.com

Booking Information:

For speeches or seminar presentations on this topic, please send an email request to Dave Arnott at davea@dbu.edu or dvarnott@gmail.com

Ordering Information:

U.S. trade bookstores and wholesalers: Please contact Dave Arnott at davea@dbu.edu or dvarnott@gmail.com

Dedication

Davey Naugle taught me everything I know
about the Christian Worldview.

Contents

Economics and the Christian Worldview

CHRISTIANITY IS dismal because we "see through a glass darkly." Economics is dismal because it is about human behavior. We will look at both of these ideas; but first, we will consider economics.

Economics

Economics is about how humans make choices related to production and distribution of products and services in scarce environments. You would think that self-interested (fallen) people would make choices that serve themselves at the expense of others. They do. But that is the providential thing about free market economics: When fallen people make self-interested choices, they serve others. Thus, Free Markets Induce Fallen People to Serve One Another. The idea comes directly from Adam Smith's *The Wealth of Nations*, "[H]e intends only his own gain; and he is in this, as in many other cases, led by an invisible hand to promote an end which was no part of his intention" (1776/2012, p. 445). Or more simply stated, "Individuals, serving their own interests, provide for the interests of all." While it sounds dismal, we are going to call it providential, and we will even refer to it as "the divine hand," although Adam Smith never used that term.

Free Markets Induce Fallen People to Serve One Another

The following statements inform our understanding of what is meant by economics. "At its core, stewardship is about making choices, and making choices is the science of economics. Making decisions that please God is our goal as God's stewards" (Bradley, 2016, p. 24). "At bottom, economics is about us—what we choose, what we value, what we represent in language and symbols, how we interact with each other in a market, and especially how we produce, exchange, and distribute goods, services, risk, and wealth" (Richards, 2010, p. 5). It is about how we conduct our lives. Jesus was involved in the production and distribution of scarce furniture.

> **Jesus was involved in the production and distribution of scarce furniture.**

We are called to "go." For some of us, that means to go be a missionary, pastor, or evangelist vocationally. For the rest of us, it can mean "as you go about" your daily lives. Our lives are economic because we continually make exchanges in a scarce environment. Your choice to read this book prevents you from doing something else. Economists call that "opportunity cost."

Economics is dismal because, as a social science, it tries to predict human behavior. Good luck with that. Let us differentiate "hard sciences" from "social sciences."

The iceberg represents what we can see and measure above the water (hard sciences) and what is more difficult to see and measure below the water (social sciences). If you see the top of an iceberg, you know it is supported by a large portion of the iceberg underwater. In a social

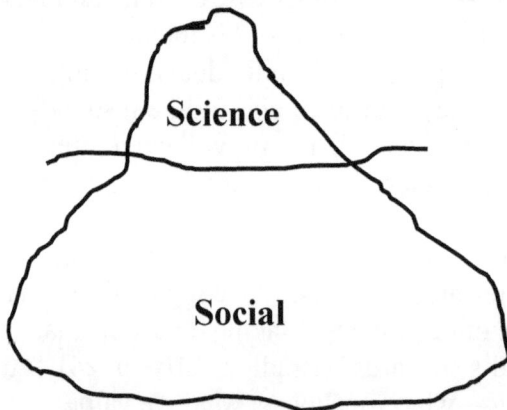

science, like economics, we are trying to measure "underwater" concepts.

In the classroom, I show the iceberg diagram and write the concept "love" below the water. Groups of students are assigned to suggest "above water" measures of love in a marriage

that adhere to the rules of science: Constructs must be measurable and replicable. Meaning, when you see a construct, and I see one, we both count it as one. Measures of the top of the iceberg could include height, width, hardness, and temperature. The best answers about love between a married couple are "the size of the diamond" and "the number of children." You are probably thinking, "Those are terrible measures!" Welcome to the dismal science.

In economics, we say people have needs. How do they satisfy those needs? Well, the interesting thing is, needs have never changed. It doesn't matter whether you believe the world is 6,000 years old or millions of years old, human needs have never changed. All the needs satisfied by the smartphone that is interrupting your reading of this book were the same needs humans had when they first appeared on earth. How they *satisfy* those needs has changed. That is what economists try to predict in our dismal science. Mark Twain was right, "Predictions are difficult, especially those about the future." They are difficult, and dismal.

In 1940, Ludwig Von Mises, in his seminal work *Human Action*, defines economics as the science of purposeful human action (1940/2008, p. 11). In our Christian context, economics is the science of making God-pleasing decisions (Bradley, 2016, p. 33). Normative economics explain how the economy *should* work. A good example is the Good Samaritan story: It explains how people *should* care for one another. Another example is, "When gas prices go up, people should drive less." These economic predictions look forward, trying to predict future behavior. When gas prices go up, people *do* drive less. How much less? That is econometrics, which is beyond the scope of this book. I concentrate mostly on direction in this brief book, not specific data measurement.

I often walk across the front of my Economics classroom and state, "Your 7th grade physical science teacher walked across the front of the classroom like this and asked you which direction she was pushing the earth." The answer is fairly simple, and it is a good way to teach Newton's third law of motion about equal and opposite forces. She was obviously pushing the earth backward from the direction she was walking. Economic "pushes" are like that. Richards states, "We *know* how poverty is alleviated and wealth is created. … What is so perplexing, and so maddening, is how many Christian thinkers seek to eradicate the remaining poverty while largely ignoring the known and well-trod path" (2014, p. 246). Economists know what causes "the wealth of nations" and "the poverty of nations." Why we continually practice more poverty than wealth is a recurring question in this book. We seek to explain how Christian economists can spread wealth, instead of poverty.

Positive economics looks back and says, "When people accept the Good Samaritan story as Jesus told it, they respond more kindly to the poor and injured." When a measure is produced that verifies that the Good Samaritan's response is the correct response, you have positive economics. With a measure that shows people reduced their driving by 5% as a result of the last gas price increase, you have positive economics. So, economics can be seen as a hard science when you look back, because the data is irrefutable. But it is typically seen as a soft (dismal) science because it tries to look forward.

> **It's the Good Samaritan story, not the Good Government story.**

Harvard economist and textbook author Gregory Mankiw served in the George Bush administration. In a March 2019 interview, he was asked by Dallas Federal Reserve Bank president Robert Kaplan, "What is the biggest misunderstanding that politicians have about economists, and that economists have about politicians?" His answer, "Politicians ask us questions we can't answer." Those are predictions about the future: What will be the response to tax cuts, tariffs, etc. "And they don't ask us questions that we *can* answer, like the effects of rent control." The biggest misunderstanding that economists have about politics? "How hard it is to change policy" (Dallas Fed, 2019). He was making the point that economics is dismal because politicians want us to predict the future, which is quite hard to do. We are better at predicting the past.

Christianity

The study of Christianity is dismal also. What did God intend? Well, if we knew that, we would be God. That is why our understanding of Biblical economics is not very accurate. It is hard for humans to know what God meant in the scriptures. We are fallen, foolish humans, stumbling around the broken earth, trying to figure out how to redeem it. John Bolt, in *Economic Shalom: A Reformed Primer on Faith, Work, and Human Flourishing* states, "There is no escape from the task of interpretation; we read and apply the Bible as fallible and finite human beings who will disagree with each other until our Lord returns" (2013, p. 12).

There is no such thing as an egotistical believer. We see things through a glass darkly. That is why Joe Galindo (2019) suggested we have "an abundance of advisors." The more views we have on a Christian subject, the better chance we have of getting to the truth. This idea is expanded in the Christian Worldview section of this chapter.

Donald A. Hay makes the following observation:

> All this may come as a disappointment to any who hoped that we would be able to give definitive "Christian answers" to economic problems. But Jesus never promised us that Christian discipleship in a fallen world would be easy: the Christian who wishes to comment on economic issues has no shortcuts available, no answers he or she can read off directly. Submission to the scriptures, intellectual humility, a willingness to listen to other Christians, and an openness to the guidance of the Holy Spirit are the qualities required. (2014, p. 63)

The father of the scientific method, Francis Bacon, said it this way, "A little philosophy inclineth man's mind to atheism; but depth in philosophy bringeth men's minds about to religion (1909, lines 3-5). When you continue learning, you get closer to God. That is where He wants you—closer to Him, knowing more about the bountiful world He made. He wants you to help Him re-create in wonderful, amazing ways a world you cannot even imagine.

So, there are two dismal sciences: Economics and Christianity. Thank you for joining this adventure to find out what we know and what we do not know. As we travel this journey together, we will seek answers to some of the most difficult questions we face.

The Christian Worldview: Creation, Fall, Redemption

Creation   **Fall**   **Redemption**

The fall. You cannot understand economics separate from the fall. If people are not fallen, there is no scarcity, and there is no economics. We believe that, in the Garden of Eden at creation, there was no scarcity because the world was created perfectly by God. Economics starts with the fall. If the fall is the problem, what is the cure? Redemption. Not only spiritual redemption by the acceptance of Jesus Christ as our personal savior, but redemption of the world through God's use of His viceroys—that's us!

> **There are 2.2 billion Christians in the world, because their worldview fits reality.**

Everyone has answers to three questions:

1. Where did we come from?
2. What is our condition?
3. What is the cure?

In the Christian worldview, our answers are the following: Creation, Fall, Redemption.

Every good story has a creational beginning, a fallen middle, and a redemptive end. Every episode of *I Love Lucy* started with sweet music and a loving caress between Lucy and Ricky Ricardo. That is creation. Then Lucy would do something crazy to create a mess, often involving her friend, Ethel. That is the fall. Somewhere between acts II and III, Ricky would utter his famous line, "Lucy, you got some 'splaining to do!'" She "splained," asked for forgiveness, and the story ended with redemption. Every good story has those three elements. Why? As Christians, we believe God imprinted that three-part outline on our hearts. We look for it in stories. When stories end badly, we are disappointed. When the "savior" defeats the bad guys and the good guys win, we turn off the TV satisfied.

Who cares about worldview? Well, just about every action you take is based on your worldview assumptions. My Dallas Baptist University (DBU) colleague, Dr. David K. Naugle says it this way in *Worldview: The History of a Concept*, "Since nothing could be of greater final importance than the way human beings understand God, themselves, the cosmos, and their place in it, it is not surprising that a worldview warfare is at the heart of the conflict between the powers of good and evil. Consequently, an in-depth look at a concept that plays such a pivotal role in human affairs seems particularly worthwhile" (2002, p. xvii).

In *The Magician's Nephew*, Book 1 in the *Chronicles of Narnia* series, C. S. Lewis writes, "For what you see and hear depends a good deal on where you are standing: It also depends on what sort of person you are" (1955/2000, p. 136). Your worldview is where you "stand." Your perspective is driven by your worldview. "Our worldview is the spectacles through which we see and interpret reality, shaping the way we relate to God, self, others, and creation on both the personal and systematic levels" (Corbett & Fikkert, 2014, pp. 79-80). Do you see humans as created beings who are hands and minds to work? Or do you see them as mouths to feed? Your answer determines your view of humans and whether there should be more, or fewer, of them. This worldview understanding drives your economic view of people. Is an increasing population better for the world or worse for the world? Hay lends the following thought to the conversation: "The concept of rational economic man ... is not inconsistent with this biblical view of fallen man, which may explain why the concept has proved so enduring in the history of economic analysis" (2004, p. 122).

In soccer, you cannot touch the ball with your hands. In basketball, you cannot touch the ball with your feet. It is important to understand what sport you are playing. If you adopt soccer rules to play basketball, you will see the world through a cloud of confusion. The reason the Christian worldview is so popular is because it fits the world we live in. Worldwide, 2.2 billion Christians believe in creation, fall, and redemption. They are playing basketball with their hands and soccer with their feet. But so often, we see people economically playing soccer with their hands and basketball with their feet. It does not work. In *Redeeming Capitalism*, Kenneth Barnes cites a study from the National Employment Law Project (NELP) that shows no historic correlation between minimum wage increase and overall employment levels (2018, p. 138). That seems impossible. He is suggesting that when the price of something (labor) is raised, people *do not* buy less. The world does not work that way. To begin a recent macroeconomics class, I asked a student named Caitlin how much she paid for the coffee she was drinking. Then I asked another student, Cayden, "If the price of coffee goes up, will Caitlin buy more or less?" Cayden correctly answered, "Less." He had been studying economics for 45 seconds, and he knew more than the researchers with the National Employment Law Project. Cayden was playing basketball with his hands; the NELP was playing basketball with its feet. Cayden expressed his understanding of the fallen nature. People will serve their own self-interest by buying more coffee when the price goes down and less coffee when the price goes up. You do not have to know the Christian worldview, nor economics, intricately to understand what Cayden understands.

I had cataract surgery on my right eye 25 years ago but I still have not had the other eye fixed. The right side of his classroom looks like a white sheet of paper. The left side looks like a manila folder, dull and yellowish. So when you ask for my perspective on a paint color, I will ask, "Which eye? I have two very different views of the world." Those who adopt the Christian worldview see the world as created perfectly by God and spoiled by human sin; and we have a command from God to help Him redeem it. Those who disagree with any of those three parts of the Christian worldview will "see" the world very differently.

Everyone has a worldview. When Bart Simpson was asked to say grace before dinner, he mumbled, "Dear god. We paid for all this stuff ourselves, so thanks for nothing!" (Simon, Swartzwelder, & Archer, 1990). That is a worldview. The Christian worldview is sometimes called the "Three-Chapter Gospel": Creation, Fall, Redemption. And without it, economics cannot exist.

Creation

God made the world perfect. In the Garden of Eden, there was work to do, but it was not painful or oppressive. Adam and Eve named animals and plants, they

> **Creation was more than a seven-day event. It continues. Each time a baby is born, creation continues.**

tended the garden, and everything was fine. "God created the world in perfect harmony and flourishing, and He was pleased," writes Anne Bradley in *Be Fruitful and Multiply* (2016, p. 12). Nothing was scarce, so there was no economics. Work only became difficult after the fall, as does everything else with which humans interact. While we're on the subject of gardening, it is worth noting that food comes first. Eating is a necessity, not a luxury. Reverend Thomas Malthus in 1798 predicted that over population would cause a food shortage and starvation. Then

> **Malthus predicted we would run out of food. Then Norman Borlaug saved a billion lives through crop improvement. Maybe humans _are_ made in the image of God.**

Norman Borlaug saved a billion lives through crop improvement. Maybe humans are made in the image of god.

"God's daily work of preserving and governing the world cannot be separated from His act of calling the world into existence," writes Albert Wolters in *Creation Regained* (2005, p. 14). Those who believe

God created the world, then flicked it off His thumb with His index finger into space are Deists. They believe there IS a God, but He is not with us anymore. Christians who believe there is a guiding and guarding God who still functions in the world make very different economic assumptions than Deists who believe we are out here on our own. If you believe God only created the world in seven days and then left us, you will support a more active monetary policy. If you believe God is active in our lives (i.e., creation continues), then you will favor some decisions made by man and some relegated to God's providence.

This gets us quickly into the politics of economics. The key question is, "When do we make decisions, and when do we rely on God's providence?" Well, if there is no active God, man has to make all of the decisions. The phrase, "God or government," comes to mind. Something is clearly wrong with the world, which is explained in the next section. If God is not immanent, it is not difficult to conclude that humans will have to make all the decisions. *Human* ingenuity, creativity, inventiveness, and entrepreneurial zeal are the engines that have improved the human condition. "And the Club of Rome thinks that we (humans) are the *enemy!*" (Bolt, p. 110, 2013). Creative humans make the world better, not worse.

> **If God is dead, Malthus was right. ...**
>
> **He was wrong.**

In the story of creation, God brought order out of chaos. A gardener does something similar when he creatively uses the materials at his disposal and rearranges them to produce additional resources for mankind (Whelchel, 2012). Humans were poor for thousands of years. In Jesus' time, estimates are that about 95% of the population was in slavery. Then in 1776, James Watt perfected the steam engine and the world got richer. That great leap ahead in technology and living standards—the scientific revolution—came about because Christianity views man as the creative steward of a rational creation, a creation we can explore and understand because we are made in the image of a rational God who formed the cosmos (Sirico, 2012). That "leap ahead" gives title to Nobel Prize-winning economist Angus Deaton's book, *The Great Escape*. We escaped poverty by the creative nature we inherited from God.

What is our role in all this? Jim Denison says it this way:

> You are on this planet for a reason. God did not make you because the world needs another human to add to the 7.7 billion already here. He made you because He has a purpose for you that no one else can fulfill. Stay faithful to the last word you heard from God and open to the next. If you will ask your Father to use you today, He will use you today. And whether you see the results or not, eternity will never be the same. (2019b, paras. 22-24)

One of Jay Richards' top ten ways for alleviating poverty is, "Encourage belief in the truth that the universe is purposeful and makes sense" (2010, p. 210). In economic terms, we were created to please God. We do so by producing and distributing goods and services that are demanded by our neighbors. We are human beings, "creatures made in the image of God, creatures placed in the context of scarcity and given a capacity to reason, create, and transcend" (Sirico, 2012, p. 31). Workers are precious resources created in the image of God who must be able to consider prayerfully, for themselves, issues of calling, stewardship, leisure and labor (Claar & Klay, 2007). Adam Smith (a deist) believed in God, so he saw this invisible hand as God's providence over human affairs, since it creates a more harmonious order than any human being could contrive. Even though Friedrich von Hayek did not see God's providence in the market, he, too, marveled at what he called its "spontaneous order" (Richards, 2010, p. 218). So both of these economists observed order. As Christians, we attribute this to God's order.

We believe God is "still around," guarding and guiding. He appointed us His viceroys, but He is still active in our economic lives. When I mentioned to my wife, Ginger, that I was struggling with the "creation is an ongoing concept," she simply replied, "Sure. Every time a baby is born, creation continues." Simple as that. The "capacity for altruism and the desire to work come from the [creational nature]" (Hay, p. 123, 2004). We were created to work, and to perform work that serves our neighbors.

> **When Hayek called the efficiency of the market "spontaneous order," he was referring to "Intelligent Design."**

In *The Second Machine Age*, Brynjolfsson and McAfee (2016) correctly point out that truck drivers will be unemployed by self-driving trucks. Then, they incorrectly assume that demand for problem-solvers is fixed because they claim the government needs to support these unemployed truck drivers. Economists call this structural unemployment. But Brynjolfsson and McAfee are not operating under Christian worldview assumptions. We assume that fallen humans have unlimited needs, and humans made in the image of God have

> **As long as the fallen nature produces unlimited wants and the creative nature has unlimited creativity, there will be unlimited employment.**

unlimited creativity. When those two concepts are intersected by policies that promote production, truck drivers will use their "image of God" creativity to solve human needs and create more value for society than they did while driving trucks. If you assume workers are not created in the image of God, you assume lay-offs hurt the economy. If you assume they have a creative nature, lay-offs improve the economy, because they force labor to move from relatively unproductive work to more productive work.

John Bolt, in *Economic Shalom*, states the following:

> If we want to see all of the seven billion plus people on planet Earth flourish, we need to ask, what is the alternative? The answer that is then given features the word *sustainability*. Very well, but does anyone really know what sustainability involves? Isn't thinking that we are even capable of knowing this just one more example of the hubris that regularly gets us into trouble? I submit that it is impossible for anyone or any group to know the limits of our terrestrial resources and imprudent to attempt to restrict responsible exploration and use of them. In the 1970s, Americans were told we would run out of oil and gas; in 2013, we are told that it is entirely possible for North America to be energy self-sufficient. New discoveries, new technologies, greater efficiencies, alternative sources of energy—the list goes on, and no one knows what the future will bring. We will only find out when we give permission to free and resourceful people to keep trying. For any group or state to arbitrarily impose limits to this human activity would be to consign the poorest of the poor to their permanent fate. All Christians should find this unacceptable. There is a deep irony in this attempt to curtail human creativity and resourcefulness. (2013, p. 172)

I was cruising the close-out aisle at Wal-Mart and dropped a to-go coffee mug in my basket. Later, I realized it was designed with a device on the bottom that prevented tip-overs. It has become one of my favorite classroom examples. Tipping coffee cups is a problem in a fallen world. A creative human solved the problem. There are unlimited problems to be solved and unlimited creativity to solve them. When mediated by policies that promote production (where people are rewarded for solving problems), there should never be an unemployed person.

> **Jimmy Carter predicted we would run out of oil in 2011. But college freshmen are paying less for gas than I did 45 years ago!**

This human creativity is expressed around us on a daily basis. The lightbulb that allows you to read this book, the chair you're sitting on, the shoes on your feet, were all made by creative human beings who improved their product offering to serve their neighbors. Even the mention of "lightbulb" probably had you asking "Incan-

> **"Polices that promote production" is all that separates rich from poor nations.**

descent or LED?" That is another example of creative humans improving a product that protects and sustains resources. "No one ever made an ounce of earth" is the first line in Fred Gottheil's *Principles of Economics* textbook." He continues, "Economists accept as fact that every resource on the face of the earth is a gift of nature" (2013, p. 3). The lightbulb, the chair, your shoes, they all came from the earth, and we humans didn't do any-

> **There's a limited amount of land, and God is not making any more. But He is making creative human beings who discover more efficient ways of using it.**

thing to create it. We simply scoop up the dirt and through God's providential guiding, find ways to create greater value for our neighbors.

God was once approached by a scientist who said, "Listen God, we've decided we don't need you anymore. These days we can clone people, transplant organs and do all sorts of things that used to be considered miraculous."

God replied, "Don't need me huh? How about we put your theory to the test. Why don't we have a competition to see who can make a human being, say, a male human being."

The scientist agrees, so God declares they should do it like He did in the good old days when He created Adam.

"Fine" says the scientist as He bends down to scoop up a handful of dirt."

"Whoa!" says God, shaking His head in disapproval. "Not so fast. You get your own dirt."

Hugh Whelchel said, "Only God can create something out of nothing.... [Our call is to] create something out of something" (2012, p. xviii). God made the dirt out of nothing. We scoop it up and make something out of it: Lightbulbs, chairs, shoes, even this book.

God creates; humans discover. We discover God's creation when we "positivize" it. The whole of creation is crying out to be positivized (Wolters, 2005, p. 44). In economics, we discover what God had in mind. The German-based company BASF has a TV advertisement that proclaims, "We create chemistry." In the Christian worldview, we believe they "discover" chemistry. The label on a bottle of Ozarka™ water reads, "Made in Texas." Really?! They *made* the water? Maybe they "discovered" the water. A Hallmark gift bag reads "We create ourselves as we go." No, we don't. God creates, we discover. I drive by Midlothian (Texas) High School every day. A marble diagram designed into the floor of the main hallway reads, "MISD: Creating a better future, one student at a time." I know what they mean, so I am not going to show up at a school board meeting and make a fuss. But we understand that God *created* the world,

> **God creates.
> Humans discover.**

we simply *discover* what He wants us to do with it. So a better statement for MISD might be, "Discovering a better future for our students." That would keep the slogan in line with the Christian worldview.

Joseph Schumpeter wrote about "creative destruction," the concept that new products and services "destroy" the old ones (2009, pp. 42-43). Computers creatively destroyed typewriters. Cre-

> **Creative destruction
> is rooted in creation,
> not the fall.**

ative destruction is rooted in creation, not the fall. Humans are created in the image of God; thus, the seed of creativity we all enjoy causes us to create new and better ways of producing value for our fellow humans. Eleven recessions have occurred since World War II. Each of the low points at the bottom of the cycle are higher than the previous nadir. Why? Because we inherited creativity from our creator. Life gets better and better when we use our God-given creative nature. If we were relying on the fallen nature, each successive nadir would be lower.

Fall

Most economic myths stem from a denial of the fallen nature. Without the fall, there is no scarcity. Without scarcity, there is no economics. You have to understand the fall to understand economics. In *The Virtues of Capitalism*, Hill and Rae (2010) recount being at a summer seminar when the leader asked, "What's not scarce?" One of them answered, "Salvation." I agree. I start my Macroeconomics class by observing what happened when my second through seventh grandchildren were born. Ginger and I did not have to manufacture more love, nor spread around the scarce element of love. So, love must not be scarce either. If salvation is because of God's love for us, that means salvation is based in love. Then, is love the only thing in the world that is not scarce? Seems like it.

> **Most economic myths stem from a denial of the fallen nature.**

> **Anything in creation can be directed either toward or away from God.**

Everything else is scarce, and it became so when Adam ate the apple. The fallen nature cursed everything and economics began. At a recent meeting with Josh McDowell, I noticed how he spent a few minutes explaining how a phone-sized modem could be set on the dashboard of a car, and people near it could get free wifi and a link to the gospel message. Then Josh spent 45 minutes railing at the curse of pornography that was being spread on smartphones. God made both the modem and the smartphone for good purposes, but fallen humans can choose to use them for good or evil. Josh explained how the modem was being used for good and the same-sized smartphone was being used for evil. That is true of just about everything. Wolters writes, "Anything in creation can be directed either toward or away from God—that is, directed either in obedience or disobedience to His law" (2005, p. 59). So Christian economists continually ask the question, "Are we using God's creation in the manner He intended (the creation nature) or to serve ourselves (the fallen nature)?

In *Christians and Economics*, Kerby Anderson states, "[O]ne of the reasons that Marxism was doomed to failure [is] because it did not take into account human sinfulness and our need for spiritual redemption" (2016, p. 5). Most economic myths stem from a denial of the fallen nature. Marxism denies the fallen nature, and thus it does not work. The book in which Marx called for the abolition of private property has been copyrighted. In *Joy at Work*, Dennis Bakke explains, "[A]fter Adam and Eve broke their relationship with God, all of life, including work, became more difficult and troublesome. For some, that is where the story ends. Mundane daily work is seen as an obligation, a burden, or even pure drudgery, rather than the joyous experience it was meant to be" (2005, p. 260). When we work hand-in-hand and understand the creational order, work is a joy, and that is Bakke's point. As Jay W. Richards states in *Money, Greed and God*: "Work did not arise from our fall into sin. The fall simply turned work into toil, since the ground would resist our efforts to cultivate it" (2010, p. 186). Humans flourish, though, when they find God's creational intent for their work, which is redeeming a broken world.

> **The book in which Marx called for the abolition of private property has been copyrighted.**

In April 2019, Facebook CEO Mark Zuckerberg called for more federal, and even global, oversight and governance of his company. The online blog, Morning Brew (who likes to abbreviate names) wrote it this way, "Zuck said he agrees with lawmakers that Facebook has too much power over what constitutes free speech" (Grant, 2019, para. 3). If the Facebook employees are not fallen, why would they need to be governed? Free speech is the reason Facebook is so popular. It is fascinating when one of the most powerful CEO's in the world admits his own employees are fallen. Europe's General Data Protection Regulation went into effect in May 2018, and Zuckerberg thinks it should become a global law.

Agnostic Jew, David Horowitz explains it this way in a radio interview, "The big problem we face in the world is us. And I think every Christian knows that. That we are sinners, that one of the protestant ideas is salvation by faith. We are so flawed in our beings, so prone to sin and temptation, that none of us deserves to get to heaven and that we can only get there by divine grace. It's a very profound idea" (2019). This agnostic Jew may understand the Christian worldview better than many Christians. Horowitz continues, "Why do we have a system of checks and balances? Because the founders

> **The big problem we face in the world is us.**

didn't trust the people, they felt they had to be restrained" (2019). You cannot understand economics without understanding the fallen nature of humans. In *Dark Agenda: The War to Destroy Christian America*, Horowitz further states, "It is also the Christian view: The post-Edenic world is a fallen place, irreparably damaged by the corruption of human hearts, so that no human agency can heal it" (2019, Chapter 10). I am continually amazed at how many people disagree with Horowitz, and they believe government can save men and women. It seems like a foolish idea.

God made fermentation so glucose could be broken into carbon dioxide and ethanol. It has been shown that a glass of wine made by the fermentation process might be good for you. The same alcohol is often used for evil. Twenty-three thousand people die each year in drunk-driving accidents. Maybe humans, created in the image of God, will perfect autonomous vehicles, and drunk driving will be eliminated because there won't be human drivers. We would see that as a redemption of the fall, but more about that in the next section.

Reflecting on the fallen nature, Father Robert Sirico, in *Defending the Free Market*, notes the issue of misplaced culpability: "Confusion arises when people see evils and mistakenly assume that getting rid of the free market will somehow magically solve the problem. Only a little reflection should reveal the error. Moving to a command-and-control economy doesn't remove lust and selfishness from the human heart. Those vices go right on thriving. Only now they are fed and cared for by some arm of the state ..." (2012, p. 87). The history of centralized "government reflects the fall, and the truth of Lord Acton's proverb: 'Power corrupts and absolute power corrupts absolutely'" (Lindsley, 2016, p. 32). We can't escape the fallen nature. Even Christians who have accepted Jesus Christ as their personal savior are fallen. So how do we view economic policies through this lens? That is what this book is about.

Roman Montero seems to think we can overcome our fallen nature. He tries to make a case for current day Christian socialism in *All Things in Common*: "This is why people are willing to give what they can and take only what they need[;] the assumption is that the individuals involved are socially bound together" (2017, p. 22). Montero is right: Where people are bound, they can practice socialism, as my wife and I

> **I bought a copy of the book, *All Things in Common*.**

do in our home, where we are bound. To assume we are bound by being Americans, or more precisely, by being in America, is a socialist assumption with which few Americans agree. People choose to be bound to one another; it is not the state's role to order people to be bound. So Montero is seeing "binding" by the government using power at the national level, where we see it working only voluntarily, at the family level.

Can we avoid the fall? "Nothing is secular," says Arthur Brooks (2019). His point is that the sacred-secular divide the Greeks first introduced and is so popular in modern culture is not God's idea. Duality is dangerous because it encourages us to keep our Lord in His glass-stained box on Sunday. That is not how the Christian worldview works. And it is not how economics works. Everything is economic (except for love), and everything is sacred. Trying to make the sacred secular is not biblical. It is a nice tradition to pray before eating a meal; but if you are thanking God for providing food, there are equally good reasons for thanking Him before you start your car, turn on your computer, or open this book. He provided all of them for you. All of them were made for a sacred purpose, but they can be used in secular ways because of the fallen nature of humans.

Nothing is secular.

This sacred-secular split is explained in a quote by the famous Dutch theologian, Abraham Kuyper: "There is not a square inch in the whole domain of our human existence over which Christ, who is Sovereign over all, does not cry: Mine!" (Bratt, 1998, p. 461). That is a favorite quote of my colleague at Dallas Baptist University, Dr. David K. Naugle, who authored the definitive book on Christian worldview, titled *Worldview: The History of a Concept*. Davey's dog is named Kuyper.

Jim Denison (2019a) explains the split this way, "You and I inherited our Western culture from the Greeks and Romans. Centuries before Christ, their worldview divided the soul from the body, determining that the former is positive while the latter is evil. This belief led centuries of Christians to venerate monastic withdrawal from the world as the highest form of spirituality" (para. 14).

This pervasive, secular idea has encouraged Christians to adopt the culture that splits Sunday churchgoing from their weekday work. The Christian worldview does not support that split. That is what this book is about: trying to determine how we integrate our Christian worldview and biblical understanding with our economic behaviors.

Examples of denying the fallen nature are plentiful. One is the Patient Protection and Affordable Care Act ("Obamacare"), which assumed people would rise above their self-interest and buy insurance, even though it was cheaper to simply pay the fine and buy the insurance once they got sick. Self-interested consumers paid the fine; and when they bought the insurance, they found that the group of insured people contained too many sick people and not enough healthy folks. When the Obamacare plan was announced, everyone who understood the Christian worldview knew it would not succeed because it denied the fallen nature. Economics is rife with these examples, leading to perhaps my most often cited truth about economics, "Most economic myths stem from a denial of the fallen nature."

A particularly bright DBU student asked us what should be done about the "gentrification" of neighborhoods. Gentrification occurs when a neighborhood moves upscale and former tenants and homeowners cannot afford to live there. If you assume the improvement in the socio-economic status of the new neighbors is a result of the fall, you would wage war against it. If you assume the improvement is a result of creation, you would encourage it. It is quite clear: Improving a neighborhood is part of creation, so we should encourage it. Now, what should be done to aid displaced families is a more difficult question, and I appreciate that my student is in the neighborhood trying to help. This is a good application of the Christian worldview and economics. When you can determine whether an effect is part of creation or the fall, you know how to proceed.

The Christian worldview seems unique in its assumption that creation and the fall are distinct events. All other belief systems seem to fall into the trap of blaming God for human mistakes. This unique assumption is what makes the Christian worldview so powerful in economics. God made a perfect world; it is we humans who have messed it up. The I-ching diagram, so popular for its yin and yang elements, says that the good is enfolded in the bad and the bad is enfolded in the good. As the wheel turns, the two get mixed up. The Christian worldview rejects that idea. The fall is a parasite on, not a part of, creation (Wolters, 2005).

Applying an understanding of the fallen nature, Christians should reject state-controlled or centrally controlled economies, which concentrate power in the hands of a few sinful individuals. Instead, we should support an economic system that disperses that power and protects us from greed and exploitation (Anderson, 2016) from fallen people. We must look to the economic system that takes men and women on their worst days and can, more often than not, get them to act in the interest of others (Lindsley & Bradley, 2017). Competition forces fallen people to serve others before they can be served.

People who favor the growth of state power don't understand the fallen nature of the people who work in govern-

> **The free market induces fallen people to serve one another.**

ment. Christians who take the reality of sin seriously, so it seems to me, ought to do the exact opposite: encourage the curtailment of state power in the hands of fallen people. In other words, we should trust free people more and powerful people—or those lusting after power—less (Bolt, 2013).

Government-controlled economies operated by fallen humans have attempted, and continue to attempt, to transform human behavior through manipulation and the elimination of trade, and the consequences are dire: great suffering and early death. Capitalism, rather than trying to change the sinner's heart, takes it as it is and uses a system of incentives to encourage service. The result is greater flourishing, better protected environments, increased wealth and well-being, and the near eradication of abject poverty (Lindsley & Bradley, 2017). When fallen humans work in a free economy, they do a far better job than socialist economies at giving greedy people socially useful ways to get rich (Witt, 2017). Fallen people can be induced to serve others when the inducements are right.

In *Roaring Lambs*, Bob Briner (1995) asks why his fellow parishioners in a small Free Methodist church in south Dallas did not encourage him to take his writing skills to Hollywood as a teenager. The obvious answer is, "It is a den of thieves. It is Sodom and Gomorrah." Briner reasonably asks, "If Christians abandon an industry, how can it be redeemed?" Good question. We are not supposed to abandon politics, business, entertainment, nor economics. It is just that the "double-dismal" science of Christian economics makes decisions about what groups to join—and which not to join—rather difficult. It does not mean we should give up and let the secular world take over. We should analyze and try to determine God's creational intent for the lives we have together in macroeconomics.

Nothing will be perfect in a fallen world. In *Money, Greed, and God*, Jay Richards writes, "[C]an't we build a just society? The answer: we should do everything we can to build a *more* just society and a more just world. And the worst way to do that is to try to create an egalitarian utopia" (2010, p. 32). What has always made the state a hell on earth has been precisely that man has tried to make it his heaven.

> **"What has always made the state a hell on earth has been precisely that man has tried to make it his heaven."**
>
> **~Johann Holderlin**

As Christian economists, we are wary of utopian plans that promise perfection. We believe our calling is to redirect our world gently. So, we do not believe in violent overthrow, and we do not believe in destroying an existing situation. A Christian called to be the economic czar of Cuba or North Korea would not destroy the existing system, she would merely redirect the scarce resources God put there. We believe God had a perfect intention, and the call of fallen humans is to make it better by gently changing the economic system. Utopian visions deny the fallen nature of humans. We can't make the world perfect, but we can make it better by aligning economic resources with God's creational intent.

Anderson comments on this issue of alignment, "Perhaps the most significant connection between Hayek and Christianity can be found in their common understanding of human nature. Hayek started with a simple premise: human beings are limited in their understanding. The

Bible would say that we are fallen creatures living in a fallen world" (2016, p. 43). Due to human fallibility, Hay notes, "There is little point in advocating for secular society economic structures which presuppose the existence of a closely knit community of love, as in the early church in Jerusalem. That would be foolish utopianism. Instead we have to look for a second best ..." (2004, p. 63).

Jay Richards writes about our human limitations in *Money, Greed, and God: Why Capitalism is the Solution and not the Problem*:

> The central point is not our greed, but the limits to our knowledge. The market is a higher-level order that vastly outstrips the knowledge of any and all of us. So capitalism doesn't need greed. At the same time, it can channel greed, which is all to the good. We should *want* a social order that channels proper self-interest as well as selfishness into socially desirable outcomes. ... That's the problem with socialism: it doesn't fit the human condition. It alienates people from their rightful self-interest and channels selfishness into socially destructive behavior like stealing, hoarding, and getting the government to steal for you. ... That's because capitalism discourages miserliness and encourages its near opposite: enterprise. (2010, pp. 122-123, 125)

When people compete in a free market capitalist system, the fallen nature is channeled into creating value for your neighbors. Therefore, as Anderson notes, "The goal of capitalism is not to change people, but to protect us from human sinfulness" (2016, p. 16). Free market capitalism is not driven by greed. It is driven by love of self that is found in Matthew 22: 37-40:

> **If you love your neighbor, you will provide products and services she demands.**
> **If you love yourself, you will make a profit while doing so.**

Jesus replied: "'Love the Lord your God with all your heart and with all your soul and with all your mind.' This is the first and greatest commandment. And the second is like it: 'Love your neighbor as yourself.' All the Law and the Prophets hang on these two command-ments." We are commanded to love ourselves. That means we care about the flourishing of others as well as ourselves.

> **Free market capitalism is not driven by greed. It's driven by love of self.**

Again, Richards points out the following:

That's the whole point of freedom it always involves costs—that is, trade-offs. To choose one path is to foreclose the opposite path [which economists call "opportunity cost."]. Even God accepted trade-offs. He chose to create a world with free beings, one that allowed those beings to turn against Him. And they did. But their freedom didn't <u>cause</u> them to choose the bad. It just <u>allowed</u> them to. So, too, with a free economy. Critics notice all the vice present in free societies. But it is only in free societies that we can fully exercise our virtue. Charity is charity, for instance, only if it's not coerced. (2010, p. 164)

Utopian Ideas Deny the Fallen Nature

As stated previously by Richards, "Can't we build a just society? The answer: we should do everything we can to build a *more* just society and a more just world. And the worst way to do that is to try to create an egalitarian utopia" (2010, p. 32). The world is not perfect, and we cannot make it that way. But we can make it better.

Society makes opportunity cost trade-offs that prove utopian schemes don't work. "The optimal level of pollution cleanup for a society is not zero. Neither is it 100 percent. The optimal level of pollution cleanup lies at the point where we decide additional cleanup is not worth the time, the trouble, and the money. We should clean up our environment until things are 'good enough' and then move on to more urgent tasks" (Claar & Klay, 2007, pp. 102-103). Those who call for a "perfect environment" deny the fallen nature. There is no perfection in a broken world. There is improvement. Bolt underscores the importance of creation as the foundation for economic thinking: "[A] normative understanding of our economic life must be rooted in creation and not in eschatology ... but as a check on perfectionist utopianism, not as a template for radical transformation of our social order" (2013, p. 19). Sirico offers the following logical—and accurate—assessment: "Recognizing that heaven on earth is impossible, we do not pursue utopian schemes" (2012, p. 176). When an economist hears the phrase "win-win," our economic antenna start to quiver.

If not perfection, then what? In *The Red Sea Rules*, Robert Morgan writes that the first rule is, "Realize that God means for you to be where you are" (2014, p. 1). You are called to re-create the economic situation you are in. God put you there for a reason, and it is your calling to figure that out. Art Lindsley writes, "You are the only *you* there ever was or ever has been" (2015, p. 80). In the movie of the same name, the Blues Brothers famously shouted, "We're on a mission from God." Are you on a mission to improve the situation you're in?

Arthur Holmes, in *The Idea of a Christian College*, writes, "What we need is not Christians who are also scholars but Christian scholars" (1987, p. 7). I agree with Holmes and echo that thought: What we need is not Christians who are economists; we need Christian economists. The title of Holmes' book is taken from *The Idea of a University* by Cardinal John Henry Newman. Seen in this light, the Christian worldview is the ballast that supports the path we walk. When we see the world through our Christian worldview lens—creation, fall, redemption—we find answers to our questions about how to distribute scarce goods in a fallen world. Though, as Whelchel states, "We will never create full shalom in this current age" (2012, p. 95). It is not a perfect world, and we cannot make it perfect. We have to settle for marginal improvements.

Milt experienced God's providence, without ever recognizing it. Almost all men marry women shorter than themselves, so this presented a problem to Milt, who was a 5-foot-tall student at the University of Chicago in 1932. As an atheist, Milt considers it a coincidence that in one of his first economics classes, he met a woman named Rose, who was shorter than him. The Christian worldview looks at the same situation and calls it "providence" that Milt and Rose met in that class. When Rose married Milton, her last name changed to Friedman, and thus, the most influential husband-wife economics team of the 20th century was created. God intended Milton and Rose Friedman to be in the same classroom at the University of Chicago in 1932. They were not Christians, but in the Christian worldview, we believe God used them to re-create His world through their economic research and teaching. What the Friedman's call "coincidence," Christians call "providence." The next time you're in a group, maybe at church, notice how many women are under 5-feet tall. Not many.

> **What others call "coincidence" Christians call "providence."**

Milton and Rose Friedman analyzed economic concepts that made the future better for all economists. We should encourage an "orientation to the future and the belief that progress but not utopia is possible in this life" (Richards, 2010, p. 210). As Lindsley states, "Left to ourselves things tend toward disorder, a loss of spiritual life, a decline in vitality" (2016, p. 1) because we have a fallen nature. Christians believe we need to find a way for fallen people to serve one another. That happens in free market systems.

The Christian worldview assumes there *is* perfection in creation, but we cannot find it because we are fallen humans with limited understanding of the world God created. But there is hope, in redemption.

Redemption

Christianity is the only religion we know of where we are "saved to behave." In all other religions, people "behave to be saved." The direction of causality is important. God is the Redeemer of the world, and He empowers us to carry on His redemptive purpose as we serve others. We need to make it clear that we do not redeem the

> **Most religions believe you must behave to be saved. Christians believe we are saved to behave.**

world to *earn our salvation.* We redeem the world *because we are saved.* In *The Cure,* Lynch, McNicol, and Thrall (2016) describe two different rooms: the room of good intentions, and the room of grace. Their thesis is the following: "You're saved. Start acting like it!" That is how the Christian worldview sees behavior. Your salvation is secure, now go out and redeem the world. "When it speaks of the Kingdom, the New Testament uses verbs like *receive, inherit, enter,* and *work.* We are called to enter into it by faith in Christ alone and to pray that we may be enabled more and more to submit ourselves to the beneficent rule of God in every area of our lives" (Whelchel, 2012, p. 26).

The understanding that we are "saved to be behave" and we do not "behave to be saved" makes a clear distinction between the economic thinking of those who hold the Christian worldview and the economic thinking of others who do not. We are saved to make the world better, but we cannot make things perfect. Thus, utopian plans are not in our wheelhouse. We cannot do it. During class, I praised the Trump administration's renegotiation of the NAFTA deal with Mexico. A bright student asked, "But it will require that a higher percentage of autos be made with expensive U.S. labor, increasing the cost to the consumer." I agreed and made the Christian worldview application, "It's not perfect, but it's better." That is what we do as Christian economists. To quote Alex Haley, "We find the good and praise it." We know perfection does not exist in a fallen earth, but we claim redemption when we make it better. That is our role—not utopian dreams of perfection, but incremental improvement. Hay reminds us that "[t]he search for second-best solutions should not, however, be allowed to erode our perception that they are only second best and not fully consistent with what God requires. In pursuing the possible, we must not forget the ideal, and there should be an element of sadness and repentance that our solutions must fall so far short of the ideal" (2004, p. 63).

> **Utopian plans are not in our wheelhouse.**

Lindsley explains redemption this way: "Redemption, above all, applies to all of life. Not only are we redeemed from our sin (personal), we are brought into a new community—the Body of Christ (corporate). Our redemption, though, extends beyond the personal and corporate to the whole cosmos. ... God's ultimate goal is the 'restoration of all things'" (Lindsley, 2016, p. 13). This means that our calling is to look at God's creation and try to discern what He wants us to do to "redeem" it.

Dennis Bakke, in *Joy at Work*, explains it this way: "Joy will be difficult to experience. It requires that we understand that the major purpose of work is to use the resources of the created world to serve our needs and the needs of others" (2005, p. 260). Bakke also states, "[T]he purpose of business ... is to steward resources with a goal of creating products and services beneficial to people" (2005, p. 259). Continuing the idea of purpose, Kotter writes about redemption like this, "Ultimately, wealth is created as people obey the cultural mandate to subdue the world and make it useful for human beings" (2015, p. 62). Thus, we poor, dumb humans are stumbling around in God's perfect creation, continually asking the question, "What did God have in mind?" How do we use these scarce resources to create value for ourselves and our fellow humans? God intends for humans to flourish, but we struggle to do so because of our fallen nature.

God did not have to include us in His redemptive mission, but because of His love for us, He requires us to help further His kingdom until Christ returns. We can only experience true joy when we do what God has designed us to do. God did not create us to run around engaging in useless, time-consuming activities to await His return. Instead, He created us to use our gifts to serve His creation, bring Him glory, and contribute to greater human flourishing. In doing this, we help bring about a state of affairs that is closer or more aligned with the way things were supposed to be as we anticipate His return (Bradley, 2016).

We are not alone in this redemption effort. God graciously guides us in fulfilling His redemptive purpose. Whelchel states, "[T]he work flowing from God's vocational call on our lives is an extension of God's work of maintaining and providing for His creation. But even more than that, it is reweaving shalom. It is a contribution to what God wants done in the world" (2012, p. 122). Lindsley notes the important implication of Christ as Redeemer—and as our example—as we seek to carry out God's redemptive work: "Christ's redemption of our lives allows us to be more and more what we are created to be" (2016, p. 1). Finding our creational intent is difficult. The intention of this little book is to help us as we attempt to find God's creational intent for our economic lives.

God has an intended purpose for us in this world. Hunter states, "[We] are enjoined to participate in ways framed by the revelation of God's word in the creative and renewing work of world-making and remaking. And it is in the divine nature of this work that vocation is imbued with great dignity" (2010, p. 93). Whelchel lends clarity to the role of work in God's plan: "We must see our work within the larger perspective of God's plan for the restoration of His creation" (Whelchel, 2012, p. 119).

Our role is clarified by Corbett and Fikkert, "[W]hile God made the world 'perfect,' He left it 'incomplete.' This means that while the world was created to be without defect, God *called* humans to interact with creation, to make possibilities into realities, and to be able to sustain ourselves via the fruits of our stewardship" (2014, p. 55). Bradley continues the thought regarding human interaction with God's creation: "We are called to be stewards of the earth. Stewardship comes from the Greek word *oikonomia*, which appears in the New Testament. It is a Greek compound word that is translated as the 'management of household affairs, stewardship, and administration.' Of course, this is where we get the term 'economics'" (Bradley, 2016, p. 23). So in economics we are called to be stewards of the earth. God called fallen people to restore the earth to His original creational intent.

> **God called fallen people to restore the earth to His original creational intent.**

How do we determine what God intended? We learn as we go. Economics is a young discipline. If Adam Smith was the founder when he wrote *The Wealth of Nations* in 1776, economics is only 244 years old. But we usually talk about the "modern era" of economics starting when Maynard Keynes wrote *The General Theory* in

1936. Friedrich von Hayek wrote *The Road to Serfdom* in 1944. We have very little data. Only 11 recessions have occurred since World War II, and only during this time period of about 80 years have we made significant economic observations. I tell my students that models may get better in their lifetime as we gain more data and economic models are refined. This reminds us of the importance of the fall in our view of redemption. If we assume humans are not fallen, we would expect perfect economic decisions. When we understand the fall, the expectation for redemption is only marginal improvements through experience.

What does this thing called redemption look like? In my hometown of Midlothian, Texas, many of my neighbors work at one of the three cement plants in the "Cement Capital of Texas." As workers excavate limestone that was left by an ocean that receded millions of years ago, they subject it to a 3,000 degree Fahrenheit furnace and turn it into cement. As a result, we have homes to live in, roads to drive on, and office buildings to work in. That is how fallen humans redeem God's creation to produce human flourishing. Here is an example from the Old Testament: "Daniel's approach to life in Babylon as a public servant meant that he sought to use his gifts through his vocational calling to transform the culture around him" (Whelchel, 2012, p. 93). He redeemed the situation God put him in.

Hugh Whelchel says it this way, "Milton Friedman said the purpose of a business is to increase value for the owners. Our owner is God" (2018). So we "serve our Owner" when we create value for our neighbors. It is not about us, it is about our neighbors. It is no use seeking salvation in institutions, programs, and projects. Röpke states, "We shall save ourselves only if more and more of us have the unfashionable courage to take counsel with our own souls and, in the midst of all this modern hustle and bustle, to bethink ourselves the firm, enduring, and proved

> **The purpose of a business is to increase value for the owners. Our owner is God.**

truths of life" (1960, p. 8). In other words, we cannot save ourselves. Anderson continues the theme: "We should not accept the idea that the state can transform people from the outside. Only the gospel can change people from the inside and so that they become new creatures (2 Corinthians 5:17)" (2016, p. 12). We notice his use of the term "creatures." That means we are made in the image of God, and as such, we should use our creative nature to redeem the fallen world back to God's creational intent.

God's creational intent was for you to have a perfect physical body. You do not have a perfect physical body because you eat too many donuts and cookies. You join with God's creational hand when you re-create your body. You call it re-creation. That is a powerful metaphor for understanding how we work hand-in-hand with God to bring redemption to the world. When you stop a fight between your small children, you are re-creating their relationship. When you teach a child how to play soccer, you are re-creating his ability. When you teach Sunday School, you are contributing to God's re-creational intent.

Fred Gottheil, in his economics textbook, *Principles of Microeconomics*, says, "[R]esources were there for the taking. And ... we took! We learned how to extract natural resources from the earth, how to fish them out of the waters, and how to harvest them from the lands. ... We transform iron ore into steel, crude petroleum into plastic, trees into furniture, rays of the sun into energy, ... sand into glass, limestone into cement, ... and water flow into electricity. We are continually discovering newer techniques for transformation" (2013, p. 3). We use existing scarce resources to re-create the earth that God created.

When I worked in pro tennis, there was a theme of "being in the flow," or "being in the zone." This came from a man named Mihaly Csikszentmihalyi. It meant the player felt he could hit the ball anywhere he wanted in any situation. Abraham Maslow called it "self-actualizing." In the movie, *Chariots of Fire*, Eric Liddell exclaimed, "When I run, I feel God's pleasure" (Puttnam & Hudson, 1981). Work feels like that when we are in line with God's creational intent. We are in the flow of God's intention for our lives. We are re-creating the world, hand-in-hand with the very Creator of the universe. As we do so, we create greater flourishing for our neighbors, as we supply their demands for products and services that improve their lives.

How do we work hand-in-hand with God? Matthew 5:14b (KJV) states, "A city that is set on a hill cannot be hid." Ronald Reagan adapted it to say, "America is a shining city upon a hill whose beacon light guides freedom-loving people everywhere." Blair Blackburn authored the book *A City on a Hill* (2014) about the Christian and patriotic emblems on the DBU campus where I teach. God built the hill. We built the city. That is how we work hand-in-hand with God.

> ## God built the hill.
> ## We built the city.

Wolters explains how Jesus "re-created" in ways we cannot:

> In connection with our theme of re-creation, it is particularly striking that all of Jesus' miracles (with the one exception of the cursing of the fig tree) are miracles of restoration—restoration to health, restoration to life, restoration to freedom from demonic possession. Jesus' miracles provide us with a sample of the meaning of redemption: a freeing of creation from the shackles of sin and evil and a reinstatement of creaturely living as intended by God. (2005, p. 75)

As Christian economists, we simply ask, "What economic policies re-create the world?" How can we act as His viceroys and marshal scarce resources that clothe the poor, feed the hungry, employ the indigent, and provide for widows and orphans? "The market is, as Hayek said, 'probably the most complex structure in the universe.' It deserves our admiration. And yet very few Christian critics … have fully understood it. Fewer still have thought of it as a stunning example of God's providence over a fallen world. … [I]t is just what we might expect of a God who, even in a fallen world, can still work all things together for good" (Richards, 2010, pp. 214-215).

So that is what we continue to ask as Christian Economists: "What did God intend?" We seek God's creational intent for taxes, for minimum wage, and many other meaningful macroeconomic questions.

> **The free market is a stunning example of how God can work all things together for good, even in a fallen world.**

In Christian worldview terms, we try to encourage human flourishing by redeeming the economy. That means bringing the economy into alignment with God's original creational intent. As fallen humans, we have trouble communing with the everlasting, sovereign, eternal God, but we try. Some of the economic rules are easier to discern than others. Some are quite clear. Others continued to be viewed "through a glass darkly."

Let's enjoy the journey as we try to interpret God's creational intent for our economy.

Imagine That: A Christian Worldview Case Study

When John Lennon sang, "Imagine no possessions," he added more to his possessions than any other song he possessed. Here is a Christian worldview analysis of the popular song, "Imagine" (Lennon, 1971, A1):

> **When John Lennon sang, "Imagine no possessions," he added more to his possessions than any other song he possessed.**

Imagine there's no heaven. Heaven and hell are the original representations of good and bad. If there is no good nor bad, how would we determine that "Imagine" is a good song, and others are bad songs? If we cannot determine good from bad, how would we know which songs to listen to, and why would we listen to "Imagine"?

It's easy if you try. No hell below us. Above us only sky. Imagine all the people living for today.

If John Lennon was "living for today," why did he record the song? And if we are "living for today," why are we denying his command by listening to a song he recorded in 1971? I am aware of the idea of mindfulness, and some of that is okay. But think about it: If you are really "living for today," you are saying, "I was taught in the past how to be 'in the present' in the future." Confused? Me too. When were you taught to be mindful? Answer: In the past. When are you going to be mindful? Answer: In the future. Why would a student "living for today" get out of bed and be in my 8:00 a.m. Econ class?! Do you think that during a break from recording the song, this might have occurred to someone? Do you suppose they all broke out laughing hysterically about spending the entire day investing themselves in the future by recording a song that instructs them to "live for today"?

Imagine there's no countries, it isn't hard to do.

If there are no countries, who would John Lennon turn to when he wanted to enforce his copyright to the song "Imagine"?

Nothing to kill or die for, and no religion too.

"No religion." We tried that—in John Lennon's lifetime. There was no religion in China when Chairman Mao's Cultural Revolution killed 60 million people, mostly by redistributing food. That was between 1958 and 1961, just ten years before Lennon recorded the song. The Soviets had no religion, which allowed Josef Stalin to kill 40 million people in John Lennon's lifetime. Maybe Lennon did

> **Mindfulness says,
> "I was taught in the past
> how to be 'in the present'
> in the future."**

not read the newspapers. In an interview conducted in September 1980, three months before his death, Lennon told *Playboy* journalist David Sheff the following: "People always got the image I was anti-Christ or anti-religion. I'm not. I'm a most religious fellow" (September, 1980, p 3). If John Lennon did not follow his own advice, why should we?

Imagine all the people living life in peace.
This little book is about the "three-chapter gospel," meaning Creation, Fall, Redemption. Many people see it as a "four-chapter gospel," adding restoration. That is when Christ returns, and John Lennon will be correct—that is when all the people will live life in peace. I hold no disagreement with the four-chapter gospel. But if we are all "living life in peace," we would not need a song to encourage us to do so, and we would not listen to "Imagine." Imagine that!

You, you may say I'm a dreamer, but I'm not the only one.
I suppose Lennon is right: A lot of people write, record, and listen to songs that make no sense. He is not the only one. By the way, that is why there are 2.2 billion Christians in the world: The Christian worldview of Creation, Fall, Redemption makes sense. That's the way the world is. Christians are not dreamers, because our worldview fits reality.

> **The Christian worldview of Creation, Fall, Redemption makes sense.**

I hope someday you'll join us, and the world will be as one.
I agree with John Lennon: In restoration, the fallen nature will be replaced by the rule of Christ. But in the meantime, we live in a fallen world, so the world will not "be as one."

Imagine no possessions, I wonder if you can.
This is the best line. By possessing the copyright to "Imagine," John Lennon gained more possessions than for any other song he possessed. Do you think there were howls of laughter among the recording crew? You have to wonder how Lennon sang this line without busting out laughing!

No need for greed or hunger.

Lennon's wish has almost come true in 2019. *The New York Times* ran an article on January 5, 2019, titled, "Why 2018 was the best year in human history!" (Kristof, 2019). In the documentary film, *The Pursuit*, Arthur Brooks states, "Two billion people have been pulled out of starvation level poverty. … What did that!?" (Brooks, Papola, Fogel, Stoner, & Lee, 2019). *The Great Escape* by Nobel Prize-winning economist Angus Deaton explains how humans escaped thousands of years of destitution-level poverty. The first line is, "Life is better now than at almost any time in history" (2015, p. 1). In *Enlightenment Now*, Steven Pinker (2019) predicts the end of global poverty in his lifetime. Here is a short answer to Arthur Brooks' question: "Free market capitalism"—people possessing goods and

> **Life is better now than at almost any time in history.**

trading them for profit, which is the exact opposite of what John Lennon called for in "Imagine."

A brotherhood of man.

Like Cain and Abel. That kind of brotherhood. Because that is the kind you can expect in a fallen world. John Lennon did not understand the fall, but he practiced it. The Beatles were only together seven years when, in September 1969, John Lennon told the group he was leaving. That kind of brotherhood. Milton and Rose Friedman said, "The key insight of Adam Smith's *Wealth of Nations* is misleadingly simple: if an exchange between two parties is voluntary, it will not take place unless both believe they will benefit from it. Most economic fallacies derive from the neglect of this simple insight, from the tendency to assume that there is a fixed pie, that one party can gain only at the expense of another" (Friedman & Friedman, 1980, p. 13). Paraphrasing the Friedmans, "Most economic myths are based on the incorrect assumption of zero-sum economics." Friedman was an atheist. I am a Christian, so I say that most economic myths stem from a denial of the fallen nature.

Imagine all the people sharing all the world.
If Lennon meant "sharing free market capitalist ideas," he was right. But we think he meant sharing goods. A volume of data shows he was wrong. Just one example for now: U.S. President Lyndon B. Johnson declared a war on poverty in 1965. In the ensuing 50 years, an estimated $5 trillion was spent to keep the poverty level unchanged. "Sharing all the world" does not improve peoples' economic condition. What does? "Policies that Promote Production." For further reading on this topic, you might read *When Helping Hurts* (Corbett & Fikkert, 2014), *Poverty, Inc.* (Miller et al., 2014), *The Poverty Cure* (Miller et al., 2012). There are many other publications that show how Lennon was wrong.

You, you may say I'm a dreamer, but I'm not the only one. I hope someday you will join us. And the world will live as one.
Lennon was right: It was a dream. When the many others who dream with him wake from their dreams, they will find what the rest of us know when we are awake: The Free Market Encourages Fallen People to Serve One Another.

Input and Output

The current split in the Supreme Court is over originalism and progressivism. Originalists say the purpose of the court is to compare the new law with the existing constitution to see if it aligns. Let's call that "input." Progressives say the purpose of the court is to measure the effect of the new law on society. Let's call that "outcomes." In *Last Call for Liberty*, Os Guinness (2018) warns that a living constitution brings death—because the humans who breathe life into it are fallen. I like his advice: Inputs (like freedom) are more important than outcomes. If the ends justify the means, there is no limit to human error.

Economists tend to focus too much on the output. When analyzing socialized medicine, most economists point out that when demand increases and supply decreases—which socialized medicine has proven to do in many countries—it results in a shortage. That is the outcome measure. But as Christians, it seems we should be more concerned about the input measure, that is, what did God intend for us to do? If we find that God commanded us to have socialized medicine, we should lobby for it no matter what the cost. We should do what is right, not what works.

Economists are far too concerned with what works. Christians are commanded to do what is right and bear the cost. As Sirico points out, "A tenacious focus on outcomes (as in redistribution to achieve income parity) inevitably leads to treating people unfairly—unequally—by taking from one who has worked and produced superfluous wealth, and giving it to one who has not" (2012, p. 108). Regarding freedom, Claar and Klay note, "The plain truth is that no nation can achieve material, cultural, and moral greatness unless it offers extensive freedom of choice to workers, consumers, producers and voters. Freedom is a worthy objective in itself" (2007, p. 35). That is, freedom is a worthy input that is often disregarded in economic analysis.

This hits at the heart of the political-economic divide. Politicians - like economists - too often do what gets them re-elected, not what is right. When we see flagrant economic mistakes made by politicians, we should ask, "Ignorance or malfeasance?" Often, the answer is, "Malfeasance." You have to think that someone in the Oregon legislature knew that rent control would lower the quality and quantity of housing when their economically foolish plan was enacted in March 2019. Why did they do it? Malfeasance. They knew the input was wrong; they did it to garner votes. They assumed Oregon voters were too economically ignorant to figure it out. Any economist who can draw demand and supply curves knows that it will end badly for the people of Oregon.

Whelchel says, "Capitalism is the tool for Shalom" (2018). Shalom in this sense means more than just peace. It means human flourishing that is consistent with God's creational intent. But what did He intend? He created a perfect world that has been broken by human sin. We are called to redeem that broken world through our economic activities as we steward scarce resources. That is the great calling of Christian economists.

References

Anderson, K. (2016). *Christians and economics: A biblical point of view.* Cambridge, OH, Christian Publishing House.

Bacon, F. (1909). Of atheism. In C. W. Eliot (Ed.), *Harvard classics, volume III, part 1: Essays, civil and moral.* Retrieved from https://www.bartleby.com/3/1/16.html

Bakke, D. W. (2005). *Joy at work: A revolutionary approach to fun on the job.* Seattle, WA: PVG.

Barnes, K. J. (2018). *Redeeming capitalism.* Grand Rapids, MI: Wm. B. Eerdmans.

Blackburn, J. B. (2014). *A city on a hill: Dallas Baptist University – An architectural history.* Dallas, TX: Dallas Baptist University.

Bolt, J. (2013). *Economic shalom: A reformed primer on faith, work, and human flourishing.* Grand Rapids, MI: Christian's Library Press.

Bradley, A. (2016). *Be fruitful and multiply: Why economics is necessary for making God-pleasing decisions.* McLean, VA: Institute for Faith, Work & Economics.

Bratt, J. D. (Ed.). (1998). *Abraham Kuyper: A centennial reader.* Grand Rapids, MI: William B. Eerdmans.

Briner, B., (1995). *Roaring lambs: A gentle plan to radically change your world.* Grand Rapids, MI: Zondervan.

Brooks, A. (2019, March 27). *Love Your Enemies.* Speech presented at Dallas Baptist University, Dallas, TX.

Brooks, A., Papola, J., Fogel, T., Stoner, S., & Lee, M. W. (Producers), & Papola, J. (Director). (2019). *The pursuit* [Documentary]. United States of America: Aspiration Entertainment.

Brynjolfsson, E., & McAfee, A. (2016). *The second machine age: Work, progress, and prosperity in a time of brilliant technologies.* New York, NY: W. W. Norton and Company.

Claar, V. V., & Klay, R. J. (2007). *Economics in Christian perspective: Theory, policy and life choices*. Downers Grove, IL, InterVarsity Press.

Corbett, S., & Fikkert, B. (2014). *When helping hurts: How to alleviate poverty without hurting the poor ... and yourself* (New ed.). Chicago, IL: Moody.

Dallas Fed. (2019, March 25). *Dallas fed global perspectives with N. Gregory Mankiw* [Video file]. Retrieved from https://www.youtube.com/watch?v=ZMSXjKP7WMM

Deaton, A. (2015). *The great escape: Health, wealth, and the origins of inequality*. Princeton, NJ: Princeton University Press.

Denison, J. (2019a, March 28). British airways jet lands in wrong country on purpose. Retrieved from https://www.denisonforum.org/columns/daily-article/british-airways-jet-lands-in-wrong-country-on-purpose/?swpmtxnonce=9189d4f42c

Denison, J. (2019b, May 7). The new royal baby and Nelson Mandela: Answering 'the call to be selfless.' Retrieved from https://www.denisonforum.org/columns/daily-article/the-new-royal-baby-and-nelson-mandela-answering-the-call-to-be-selfless/

Friedman, M., & Friedman, R. (1980). *Free to choose: A personal statement*. Orlando, FL: Harcourt.

Galindo, J. (2019, March 22). *What the Bible says about business*. Paper presented at the meeting of the Lion's Den DFW Conference, Dallas Baptist University, Dallas, TX.

Gottheil, F. M. (2013). *Principles of microeconomics* (7th ed.). Mason, OH: South-Western Cengage Learning.

Grant, K. (2019, March 31). Zuckerberg: Regulate me [web log post]. Retrieved from https://www.morningbrew.com/stories/zuckerberg-regulate-me/

Guinness, O. (2018). *Last call for liberty: How America's genius for freedom has become its greatest threat*. Downers Grove, IL: IVP Books.

Hay, D. A. (2004). *Economics today: A Christian critique*. Vancouver, British Columbia: Regent College Publishing.

Hill, A., & Rae, S. (2010). *The virtues of capitalism: A moral case for free markets*. Chicago, IL: Northfield.

Holmes, A. F. (1987). *The idea of a Christian college* (Rev. ed.). Grand Rapids, MI: Wm. B. Eerdmans.

Horowitz, D. (2019). *Dark agenda: The war to destroy Christian America* [Kindle]. Available from Amazon.com

Horowitz, D. (2019, March 15). David Horowitz discusses: Dark agenda the war to destroy Christian America (S. Rios, interviewer) [Audio file]. Retrieved from https://afr.net/podcasts/sandy-rios-in-the-morning/2019/march/david-horowitz-discusses-dark-agenda-the-war-to-destroy-christian-america/

Hunter, J. D. (2010). *To change the world: The irony, tragedy, & possibility of Christianity in the late modern world.* New York, NY: Oxford Press.

Kotter, D. (2015). Remember the poor: A New Testament perspective on the problems of poverty, riches, and redistribution. In A. Bradley & A. Lindsley (Eds.), *For the least of these: A biblical answer to poverty* (pp. 57-78). Grand Rapids, MI: Zondervan.

Kristof, N. (2019, January 5). Why 2018 was the best year in human history! *The New York Times.* Retrieved from https://www.nytimes.com/

Lennon, J., & Ono, Y. (1971). Imagine [Recorded by J. Lennon]. On *Imagine* [Album]. London, England: Apple Records.

Lewis, C. S. (2000). *The magician's nephew* (Collector's ed.). New York, NY: HarperCollins Children's Books. (Original work published in 1955)

Lindsley, A. (2015). Does God require the state to redistribute wealth? In A. Bradley & A. Lindsley (Eds.), *For the least of these: A biblical answer to poverty* (pp. 79-94). Grand Rapids, MI: Zondervan.

Lindsley, A. (2016). *Free indeed: Living life in light of the biblical view of freedom.* McLean, VA: Institute for Faith, Work & Economics.

Lindsley, A., & Bradley, A. R. (Eds.). (2017). *Counting the cost: Christian perspectives on capitalism.* Abilene, TX: Abilene Christian University Press.

Miller, M. M., Fitzgerald Jr., J. F., Münkel, A., Witt, J., & Weber, M. (Producers), & Miller, M. M. (Director). (2012). *The poverty cure: Charity, justice, human flourishing* [DVD series]. United States of America: Acton Institute.

Miller, M. M., Weber, M., Fitzgerald Jr., J. F., Mauren, K., & Münkel, A. (Producers), & Miller, M. M. (Director). (2014). *Poverty, Inc.* [Documentary]. United States of America: Acton Institute.

Mises, L. V. (2008). *Human action: A treatise on economics* (Scholar's ed.). Auburn, AL: Ludwig von Mises Institute. (Original work published 1940)

Lynch, J., McNicol, B., & Thrall, B. (2016). *The cure: What if God isn't who you think He is and neither are you?* (3rd ed.). Phoenix, AZ: Trueface.

Montero, R. A. (2017). *All things in common: The economic practices of the early Christians.* Eugene, OR: Resource Publications.

Morgan, R. J. (2014). *The red sea rules: 10 God-given strategies for difficult times.* Nashville, TN: W Publishing.

Naugle, D. K. (2002). *Worldview: The history of a concept.* Grand Rapids, MI: Wm. B. Eerdmans.

Pinker, S. (2019). *Enlightenment now: The case for reason, science, humanism, and progress.* New York, NY: Penguin Books.

Puttnam, D. (Producer), & Hudson, H. (Director). (1981). *Chariots of fire* [Motion picture]. United Kingdom: 20th Century Fox (International) &Warner Brothers (United States/Canada).

Richards, J. W. (2010). *Money, greed, and God: Why capitalism is the solution and not the problem.* New York, NY: HarperCollins.

Richards, J. W. (2015). Conclusion. In A. Bradley & A. Lindsley (Eds.), *For the least of these: A biblical answer to poverty* (pp. 245-252). Grand Rapids, MI: Zondervan.

Röpke, W. (1960). *A humane economy: The social framework of the free market.* Washington, DC: Henry Regnery Company.

Schumpeter, J. A. (2009). *Can capitalism survive? Creative destruction and the future of the global economy.* New York, NY: HarperCollins.

Simon, S., Swartzwelder, J. (Writers), & Archer, W. (Director). (1990, November 1). Two cars in every garage and three eyes on every fish [*The Simpsons*]. In M. Groening (Producer). Los Angeles, CA: Fox Broadcasting Company.

Sirico, R. (2012). *Defending the free market: The moral case for a free economy.* Washington, DC: Regnery Publishing.

Smith, A. (2012). *The wealth of nations.* M. G. Spencer (Ed.). Ware, England: Wordsworth Editions Limited. (Original work published 1776)

Whelchel, H. (2012). *How then should we work?* McLean, VA: Institute for Faith, Work & Economics.

Whelchel, H. (2018, October 14). *Counting the cost: Is capitalism sustainable?* Lecture presented at the Friday Symposium, Dallas Baptist University, Dallas, TX.

Witt, J. (2017). Capitalism and the cultural wasteland. In A. Lindsley & A. R. Bradley (Eds.), *Counting the cost: Christian perspectives on capitalism* (pp. 331-363). Abilene, TX: Abilene Christian University Press.

Wolters, A. M. (2005). *Creation regained: Biblical basics for a reformational worldview* (2nd ed.). Grand Rapids, MI: Wm. B. Eerdmans.